Clement of Alexandria
Salvation of the Rich Man

Clement of Alexandria
Salvation of the Rich Man

Clement of Alexandria
Salvation of the Rich Man

© Lighthouse Publishing 2018

All rights reserved. Without limiting the rights under copyright reserved above, no part of this publication may be reproduced, stored in a retrieval system, or transmitted, in any form or by any means (electronic, mechanical, photocopying, recording or otherwise), without the prior written permission of the copyright owner of this book.

Published by
Lighthouse Christian Publishing
SAN 257-4330
5531 Dufferin Drive
Savage, Minnesota, 55378
United States of America

www.lighthousechristianpublishing.com

Introductory Note on Clement of Alexandria

[a.d. 153–193–217.] The second century of illumination is drawing to a close, as the great name of this Father comes into view, and introduces us to a new stage of the Church's progress. From Britain to the Ganges it had already made its mark. In all its Oriental identity, we have found it vigorous in Gaul and penetrating to other regions of the West. From its primitive base on the Orontes, it has extended itself to the deltas of the Nile; and the Alexandria of Apollos and of St. Mark has become the earliest seat of Christian learning. There, already, have the catechetical schools gathered the finest intellectual trophies of the Cross; and under the aliment of its library springs up something like a Christian university.

Pantænus, "the Sicilian bee" from the flowery fields of Enna, comes to frame it by his industry, and store it with the sweets of his eloquence and wisdom. Clement, who had followed Tatian to the East, tracks Pantænus to Egypt, and comes with his Attic scholarship to be his pupil in the school of Christ. After Justin and Irenæus, he is to be reckoned the founder of Christian literature; and it is noteworthy how sublimely he begins to treat Paganism as a creed outworn, to be dismissed with contempt, rather than seriously wrestled with any longer.

His merciless exposure of the entire system of "lords many and gods many," seems to us, indeed, unnecessarily offensive. Why not spare us such details? But let us reflect, that, if such are our Christian instincts of delicacy, we owe it to this great reformer in no small proportion. For not content to show the Pagans that the very atmosphere was polluted by their mythologies, so that Christians, turn which way they would, must encounter pestilence, he becomes the ethical philosopher of Christians; and while he proceeds to dictate, even in minute details, the transformations to which the faithful must subject themselves in order "to escape the pollutions of the world," he sketches in outline the reformations which the Gospel imposes on society, and which nothing but the Gospel has ever enabled mankind to realize. "For with a celerity unsurpassable, and a benevolence to which we have ready access," says Clement, "the Divine Power hath filled the universe with the seed of salvation." Socrates and Plato had talked sublimely four hundred years before; but Lust and Murder were yet the gods of Greece, and men and women were like what they worshipped. Clement had been their disciple; but now, as the disciple of Christ, he was to exert a power over men and manners, of which they never dreamed.

Alexandria becomes the brain of Christendom: its heart was yet beating at Antioch, but the West was still receptive only, its hands and arms stretched forth towards the sunrise for further enlightenment. From the East it had obtained the Scriptures and their authentication, and from the same source was deriving the canons, the liturgies, and the creed of Christendom. The universal language of Christians is Greek. To a pagan emperor who had outgrown the ideas of Nero's time, it was no longer Judaism; but it was not less an Oriental superstition, essentially Greek in its features and its dress. "All the churches of the West," says the historian of Latin Christianity, "were Greek religious colonies. Their language was Greek, their organization Greek, their writers Greek, their Scriptures and their ritual were Greek. Through Greek, the communications of the churches of the West were constantly kept up with the East. . . . Thus the Church at Rome was but one of a confederation of Greek religious republics founded by Christianity." Now this confederation was the Holy Catholic Church.

Every Christian must recognize the career of Alexander, and the history of his empire, as an immediate precursor of the Gospel. The patronage of letters by the Ptolemies at Alexandria, the translation of the Hebrew Scriptures into the dialect of the Hellenes, the creation of a new terminology in the language of the Greeks, by which ideas of faith and of truth might find access to the mind of a heathen world, —these were preliminaries to the preaching of the Gospel to mankind, and to the composition of the New Testament of our Lord and Savior. He Himself had prophetically visited Egypt, and the idols were now to be removed before his presence. There a powerful Christian school was to make itself felt for ever in the definitions of orthodoxy; and in a new sense was that prophecy to be understood, "Out of Egypt have I called my Son."

The genius of Apollos was revived in his native city. A succession of doctors was there to arise, like him, "eloquent men, and mighty in the Scriptures." Clement tells us of his masters in Christ, and how, coming to Pantænus, his soul was filled with a deathless element of divine knowledge. He speaks of the apostolic tradition as received through his teachers hardly at second-hand. He met in that school, no doubt, some, at least, who recalled Ignatius and Polycarp; some, perhaps, who as children had heard St. John when he could only exhort his congregations to "love one another." He could afterwards speak of himself as in the next succession after the apostles.

He became the successor of Pantænus in the catechetical school, and had Origen for his pupil, with other eminent men. He was also ordained a presbyter. He seems to have compiled his *Stromata* in the reigns of Commodus and Severus. If, at this time, he was about forty years of age, as seems likely, we must conceive of his birth at Athens, while

Antoninus Pius was emperor, while Polycarp was yet living, and while Justin and Irenæus were in their prime.

Alexander, bishop of Jerusalem, speaks of Clement, in turn, as his master: "for we acknowledge as fathers those blessed saints who are gone before us, and *to whom we shall go after a little time* the truly blest Pantænus, I mean, and the holy Clemens, my teacher, who was to me so greatly useful and helpful." St. Cyril of Alexandria calls him "a man admirably learned and skilful, and one that searched to the depths all the learning of the Greeks, with an exactness rarely attained before." So Theodoret says, "He surpassed all others, and *was a holy man.*" St. Jerome pronounces him the most learned of all the ancients; while Eusebius testifies to his theological attainments, and applauds him as an "incomparable master of Christian philosophy." But the rest shall be narrated by our translator, Mr. Wilson.

The following is the original Introductory Notice: —

Titus Flavius Clemens, the illustrious head of the Catechetical School at Alexandria at the close of the second century, was originally a pagan philosopher. The date of his birth is unknown. It is also uncertain whether Alexandria or Athens was his birthplace.

On embracing Christianity, he eagerly sought the instructions of its most eminent teachers; for this purpose travelling extensively over Greece, Italy, Egypt, Palestine, and other regions of the East. Only one of these teachers (who, from a reference in the *Stromata*, all appear to have been alive when he wrote) can be with certainty identified, viz., Pantænus, of whom he speaks in terms of profound reverence, and whom he describes as the greatest of them all. Returning to Alexandria, he succeeded his master Pantænus in the catechetical school, probably on the latter departing on his missionary tour to the East, somewhere about a.d. 189. He was also made a presbyter of the Church, either then or somewhat later. He continued to teach with great distinction till a.d. 202, when the persecution under Severus compelled him to retire from Alexandria. In the beginning of the reign of Caracalla we find him at Jerusalem, even then a great resort of Christian, and especially clerical, pilgrims. We also hear of him travelling to Antioch, furnished with a letter of recommendation by Alexander, bishop of Jerusalem. The close of his career is covered with obscurity. He is supposed to have died about a.d. 220.

Among his pupils were his distinguished successor in the Alexandrian school, Origen, Alexander bishop of Jerusalem, and, according to Baronius, Combefisius, and Bull, also Hippolytus.

The above is positively the sum of what we know of Clement's history.

His three great works, *The Exhortation to the Heathen* (λόγος ὁ προτρεπτικὸς πρὸς Ἕλληνας), *The Instructor, or Pædagogus* (παιδαγωγός), *The Miscellanies*, or *Stromata* (Στρωματεῖς), are among the most valuable remains of Christian antiquity, and the largest that belong to that early period.

The Exhortation, the object of which is to win pagans to the Christian faith, contains a complete and withering exposure of the abominable licentiousness, the gross imposture and sordidness of paganism. With clearness and cogency of argument, great earnestness and eloquence, Clement sets forth in contrast the truth as taught in the inspired Scriptures, the true God, and especially the personal Christ, the living Word of God, the Savior of men. It is an elaborate and masterly work, rich in felicitous classical allusion and quotation, breathing throughout the spirit of philosophy and of the Gospel, and abounding in passages of power and beauty.

The *Pædagogus, or Instructor*, is addressed to those who have been rescued from the darkness and pollutions of heathenism, and is an exhibition of Christian morals and manners, —a guide for the formation and development of Christian character, and for living a Christian life. It consists of three books. It is the grand aim of the whole work to set before the converts Christ as the only Instructor, and to expound and enforce His precepts. In the first book Clement exhibits the person, the function, the means, methods, and ends of the Instructor, who is the Word and Son of God; and lovingly dwells on His benignity and philanthropy, His wisdom, faithfulness, and righteousness.

The second and third books lay down rules for the regulation of the Christian, in all the relations, circumstances, and actions of life, entering most minutely into the details of dress, eating, drinking, bathing, sleeping, etc. The delineation of a life in all respects agreeable to the Word, a truly Christian life, attempted here, may, now that the Gospel has transformed social and private life to the extent it has, appear unnecessary, or a proof of the influence of ascetic tendencies. But a code of Christian morals and manners (a sort of "whole duty of man" and manual of good breeding combined) was eminently needed by those whose habits and characters had been molded under the debasing and polluting influences of heathenism; and who were bound, and were aiming, to shape their lives according to the principles of the Gospel, in the midst of the all but incredible licentiousness and luxury by which society around was incurably tainted. The disclosures which Clement, with solemn sternness, and often with caustic wit, makes of the prevalent voluptuousness and vice, form a very valuable contribution to our knowledge of that period.

The full title of the *Stromata*, according to Eusebius and Photius, was Τίτου Φλαυίου Κλήμεντος τῶν κατὰ τὴν ἀληθῆ φιλοσοφίαν γνωστικῶν ὑπομνημάτων στρωματεῖς— "Titus Flavius Clement's miscellaneous collections of speculative (gnostic) notes bearing upon the true philosophy." The aim of the work, in accordance with this title, is, in opposition to Gnosticism, to furnish the materials for the construction of a true gnosis, a Christian philosophy, on the basis of faith, and to lead on to this higher knowledge those who, by the discipline of the Pædagogus, had been trained for it. The work consisted originally of eight books. The eighth book is lost; that which appears under this name has plainly no connection with the rest of the *Stromata*. Various accounts have been given of the meaning of the distinctive word in the title (Στρωματεύς); but all agree in regarding it as indicating the miscellaneous character of its contents. And they are very miscellaneous. They consist of the speculations of Greek philosophers, of heretics, and of those who cultivated the true Christian gnosis, and of quotations from sacred Scripture. The latter he affirms to be the source from which the higher Christian knowledge is to be drawn; as it was that from which the germs of truth in Plato and the Hellenic philosophy were derived. He describes philosophy as a divinely ordered preparation of the Greeks for faith in Christ, as the law was for the Hebrews; and shows the necessity and value of literature and philosophic culture for the attainment of true Christian knowledge, in opposition to the numerous body among Christians who regarded learning as useless and dangerous. He proclaims himself an eclectic, believing in the existence of fragments of truth in all systems, which may be separated from error; but declaring that the truth can be found in unity and completeness only in Christ, as it was from Him that all its scattered germs originally proceeded. The *Stromata* are written carelessly, and even confusedly; but the work is one of prodigious learning, and supplies materials of the greatest value for understanding the various conflicting systems which Christianity had to combat.

It was regarded so much as the author's great work, that, on the testimony of Theodoret, Cassiodorus, and others, we learn that Clement received the appellation of Στρωματεύς (the Stromatist). In all probability, the first part of it was given to the world about a.d. 194. The latest date to which he brings down his chronology in the first book is the death of Commodus, which happened in a.d. 192; from which Eusebius concludes that he wrote this work during the reign of Severus, who ascended the imperial throne in a.d. 193, and reigned till a.d. 211. It is likely that the whole was composed ere Clement quitted Alexandria in a.d. 202. The publication of the *Pædagogus* preceded by a short time that of the *Stromata;* and the *Cohortatio* was written a short time before the *Pædagogus*, as is clear from statements made by Clement himself.

So multifarious is the erudition, so multitudinous are the quotations and the references to authors in all departments, and of all countries, the most of whose works have perished, that the works in question could only have been composed near an extensive library—hardly anywhere but in the vicinity of the famous library of Alexandria. They are a storehouse of curious ancient lore, —a museum of the fossil remains of the beauties and monstrosities of the world of pagan antiquity, during all the epochs and phases of its history. The three compositions are really parts of one whole. The central connecting idea is that of the Logos—the Word—the Son of God; whom in the first work he exhibits drawing men from the superstitions and corruptions of heathenism to faith; in the second, as training them by precepts and discipline; and in the last, as conducting them to that higher knowledge of the things of God, to which those only who devote themselves assiduously to spiritual, moral, and intellectual culture can attain. Ever before his eye is the grand form of the living personal Christ, —the Word, who "was with God, and who was God, but who became man, and dwelt among us."

Of course there is throughout plenty of false science, and frivolous and fanciful speculation.

Who is the rich man that shall be saved? (τίς ὁ σωζόμενος πλούσιος;) is the title of a practical treatise, in which Clement shows, in opposition to those who interpreted our Lord's words to the young ruler as requiring the renunciation of worldly goods, that the disposition of the soul is the great essential. Of other numerous works of Clement, of which only a few stray fragments have been preserved, the chief are the eight books of *The Hypotyposes*, which consisted of expositions of all the books of Scripture. Of these we have a few undoubted fragments. *The Adumbrations*, or *Commentaries on some of the Catholic Epistles*, and *The Selections from the Prophetic Scriptures*, are compositions of the same character, as far as we can judge, as *The Hypotyposes*, and are supposed by some to have formed part of that work.

Other lost works of Clement are: —
> The Treatise of Clement, the Stromatist, on the Prophet Amos.
> On Providence.
> Treatise on Easter.
> On Evil-speaking.
> Discussion on Fasting.
> Exhortation to Patience; or, To the newly baptized.
> Ecclesiastical Canon; or, Against the Judaizers.
> Different Terms.

The following are the names of treatises which Clement refers to as written or about to be written by him, but of which otherwise we have no trace or mention: —*On First Principles; On Prophecy; On the Allegorical Interpretation of Members and Affections when ascribed to God; On Angels; On the Devil; On the Origin of the Universe; On the Unity and Excellence of the Church; On the Offices of Bishops, Presbyters, Deacons, and Widows; On the Soul; On the Resurrection; On Marriage; On Continence; Against Heresies.*

Preserved among Clement's works is a fragment called *Epitomes of the Writings of Theodotus, and of the Eastern Doctrine*, most likely abridged extracts made by Clement for his own use, and giving considerable insight into Gnosticism.

Clement's quotations from Scripture are made from the Septuagint version, often inaccurately from memory, sometimes from a different text from what we possess, often with verbal adaptations; and not rarely different texts are blended together.

The works of Clement present considerable difficulties to the translator; and one of the chief is the state of the text, which greatly needs to be expurgated and amended. For this there are abundant materials, in the copious annotations and disquisitions, by various hands, collected together in Migne's edition; where, however, corruptions the most obvious have been allowed to remain in the text.

The publishers are indebted to Dr. W. L. Alexander for the poetical translations of the Hymns of Clement.

M. AURELIUS CASSIODORUS (WHOSE NAME IS ALSO SENATOR) WAS AN AUTHOR AND PUBLIC MAN OF THE SIXTH CENTURY, AND A VERY VOLUMINOUS WRITER. HE WOULD SHINE WITH A GREATER LUSTRE WERE HE NOT SO NEARLY LOST IN THE BRIGHTER LIGHT OF BOËTHIUS, HIS ILLUSTRIOUS CONTEMPORARY. AFTER THE DEATH OF HIS PATRON, THEODORIC, HE CONTINUED FOR A TIME IN THE PUBLIC SERVICE, AND IN HIGH POSITIONS, BUT, AT SEVENTY YEARS OF AGE, BEGAN ANOTHER CAREER, AND FOR TWENTY YEARS DEVOTED HIMSELF TO LETTERS AND THE PRACTICE OF PIETY IN A MONASTERY WHICH HE ESTABLISHED IN THE NEOPOLITAN KINGDOM, NEAR HIS NATIVE SQUILLACE. DIED ABOUT A.D. 560.] COMMENTS, I.E., *ADUMBRATIONES*. CASSIODORUS SAYS THAT HE HAD IN HIS TRANSLATION CORRECTED WHAT HE CONSIDERED ERRONEOUS IN THE ORIGINAL. SO FELL STATES: AND HE IS ALSO INCLINED TO BELIEVE THAT THESE FRAGMENTS ARE FROM CLEMENT'S LOST WORK, THE ὙΠΟΤΥΠΩΣΕΙΣ, OF WHICH HE BELIEVES *THE ADUMBRATIONES* OF CASSIODORUS TO BE A TRANSLATION.

SALVATION OF THE RICH MAN.

WHO IS THE RICH MAN THAT SHALL BE SAVED?

I. Those who bestow laudatory addresses on the rich appear to me to be rightly judged not only flatterers and base, in vehemently pretending that things which are disagreeable give them pleasure, but also godless and treacherous; godless, because neglecting to praise and glorify God, who is alone perfect and good, "of whom are all things, and by whom are all things, and for whom are all things," they invest with divine honors men wallowing in an execrable and abominable life, and, what is the principal thing, liable on this account to the judgment of God; and treacherous, because, although wealth is of itself sufficient to puff up and corrupt the souls of its possessors, and to turn them from the path by which salvation is to be attained, they stupefy them still more, by inflating the minds of the rich with the pleasures of extravagant praises, and by making them utterly despise all things except wealth, on account of which they are admired; bringing, as the saying is, fire to fire, pouring pride on pride, and adding conceit to wealth, a heavier burden to that which by nature is a weight, from which somewhat ought rather to be removed and taken away as being a dangerous and deadly disease. For to him who exalts and magnifies himself, the change and downfall to a low condition succeeds in turn, as the divine word teaches. For it appears to me to be far kinder, than basely to flatter the rich and praise them for what is bad, to aid them in working out their salvation in every possible way; asking this of God, who surely and sweetly bestows such things on His own children; and thus by the grace of the Savior healing their souls, enlightening them and leading them to the attainment of the truth; and whosoever obtains this and distinguishes himself in good works shall gain the prize of everlasting life. Now prayer that runs its course till the last day of life needs a strong and tranquil soul; and the conduct of life needs a good and righteous disposition, reaching out towards all the commandments of the Savior.

II. Perhaps the reason of salvation appearing more difficult to the rich than to poor men, is not single but manifold. For some, merely hearing, and that in an off-hand way, the utterance of the Savior, "that it is easier for a camel to go through the eye of a needle than for a rich man to enter into the kingdom of heaven," despair of themselves as not destined to live, surrender all to the world, cling to the present life as if it alone was left to them, and so diverge more from the way to the life to come, no longer inquiring either whom the Lord and Master calls rich, or how that which is impossible to man becomes possible to God. But others rightly and adequately comprehend this, but attaching slight importance to the works which tend to salvation, do not make the requisite preparation for attaining to the objects of their hope. And I affirm both of these things of the rich who have learned both the Savior's power and His glorious salvation. With those who are ignorant of the truth I have little concern.

III. Those then who are actuated by a love of the truth and love of their brethren, and neither are rudely insolent towards such rich as are called, nor, on the other hand, cringe to them for their own avaricious ends, must first by the word relieve them of their groundless despair, and show with the requisite explanation of the oracles of the Lord that the inheritance of the kingdom of heaven is not quite cut off from them if they obey the commandments; then admonish them that they entertain a causeless fear, and that the Lord gladly receives them, provided they are willing; and then, in addition, exhibit and teach how and by what deeds and dispositions they shall win the objects of hope, inasmuch as it is neither out of their reach, nor, on the other hand, attained without effort; but, as is the case with athletes—to compare things small and perishing with things great and immortal—let the man who is endowed with worldly wealth reckon that this depends on himself. For among those, one man, because he despaired of being able to conquer and gain crowns, did not give in his name for the contest; while another, whose mind was inspired with this hope, and yet did not submit to the appropriate labors, and diet, and exercises, remained uncrowned, and was balked in his expectations. So also let not the man that has been invested with worldly wealth proclaim himself excluded at the outset from the Savior's lists, provided he is a believer and one who contemplates the greatness of God's philanthropy; nor let him, on the other hand, expect to grasp the crowns of immortality without struggle and effort, continuing untrained, and without contest. But let him go and put himself under the Word as his trainer, and Christ the President of the contest; and for his prescribed food and drink let him have the New Testament of the Lord; and for exercises, the commandments; and for elegance and ornament, the fair dispositions, love, faith, hope, knowledge of the truth, gentleness, meekness, pity, gravity: so that, when by the last trumpet the signal shall be given for the race and departure hence, as from the stadium of life, he may with a good conscience present himself victorious before the Judge who confers the rewards, confessedly worthy of the Fatherland on high, to which he returns with crowns and the acclamations of angels.

IV. May the Savior then grant to us that, having begun the subject from this point, we may contribute to the brethren what is true, and suitable, and saving, first touching the hope itself, and, second, touching the access to the hope. He indeed grants to those who beg, and teaches those who ask, and dissipates ignorance and dispels despair, by introducing again the same words about the rich, which become their own interpreters and infallible expounders. For there is nothing like listening again to the very same statements, which till now in the Gospels were distressing you, hearing them as you did without examination, and erroneously through puerility: "And going forth into the way, one approached and kneeled, saying,

Good Master, what good thing shall I do that I may inherit everlasting life? And Jesus saith, Why callest thou Me good? There is none good but one, *that is*, God. Thou knowest the commandments. Do not commit adultery, Do not kill, Do not steal, Do not bear false witness, Defraud not, Honor thy father and thy mother. And he answering saith to Him, All these have I observed. And Jesus, looking upon him, loved him, and said, One thing thou lackest. If thou wouldest be perfect, sell what thou hast and give to the poor, and thou shall have treasure in heaven: and come, follow Me. And he was sad at that saying, and went away grieved: for he was rich, having great possessions. And Jesus looked around about, and said to His disciples, How hardly shall they that have riches enter into the kingdom of God! And the disciples were astonished at His words. But Jesus answereth again, and saith unto them, Children, how hard is it for them that trust in riches to enter into the kingdom of God! More easily shall a camel enter through the eye of a needle than a rich man into the kingdom of God. And they were astonished out of measure, and said, Who then can be saved? And He, looking upon them, said, What is impossible with men is possible with God. For with God all things are possible. Peter began to say to Him, Lo, we have left all and followed Thee. And Jesus answered and said, Verily I say unto you, Whosoever shall leave what is his own, parents, and brethren, and possessions, for My sake and the Gospel's, shall receive a hundred-fold now in this world, lands, and possessions, and house, and brethren, with persecutions; and in the world to come is life everlasting. But many that are first shall be last, and the last first."

V. These things are written in the Gospel according to Mark; and in all the rest correspondingly; although perchance the expressions vary slightly in each, yet all show identical agreement in meaning. But well knowing that the Savior teaches nothing in a merely human way, but teaches all things to His own with divine and mystic wisdom, we must not listen to His utterances carnally; but with due investigation and intelligence must search out and learn the meaning hidden in them. For even those things which seem to have been simplified to the disciples by the Lord Himself are found to require not less, even more, attention than what is expressed enigmatically, from the surpassing superabundance of wisdom in them. And whereas the things which are thought to have been explained by Him to those within—those called by Him the children of the kingdom—require still more consideration than the things which seemed to have been expressed simply, and respecting which therefore no questions were asked by those who heard them, but which, pertaining to the entire design of salvation, and to be contemplated with admirable and supercelestial depth of mind, we must not receive superficially with our ears, but with application of the mind to the very spirit of the Savior, and the unuttered meaning of the declaration.

VI. For our Lord and Savior was asked pleasantly a question most appropriate for Him, —the Life respecting life, the Savior respecting salvation, the Teacher respecting the chief doctrines taught, the Truth respecting the true immortality, the Word respecting the word of the Father, the Perfect respecting the perfect rest, the Immortal respecting the sure immortality. He was asked respecting those things on account of which He descended, which He inculcates, which He teaches, which He offers, in order to show the essence of the Gospel, that it is the gift of eternal life. For He foresaw as God, both what He would be asked, and what each one would answer Him. For who should do this more than the Prophet of prophets, and the Lord of every prophetic spirit? And having been called "good," and taking the starting note from this first expression, He commences His teaching with this, turning the pupil to God, the good, and first and only dispenser of eternal life, which the Son, who received it of Him, gives to us.

VII. Wherefore the greatest and chiefest point of the instructions which relate to life must be implanted in the soul from the beginning, —to know the eternal God, the giver of what is eternal, and by knowledge and comprehension to possess God, who is first, and highest, and one, and good. For this is the immutable and immoveable source and support of life, the knowledge of God, who really is, and who bestows the things which really are, that is, those which are eternal, from whom both being and the continuance of it are derived to other beings. For ignorance of Him is death; but the knowledge and appropriation of Him, and love and likeness to Him, are the only life.

VIII. He then who would live the true life is enjoined first to know Him "whom no one knows, except the Son reveal (Him)." Next is to be learned the greatness of the Savior after Him, and the newness of grace; for, according to the apostle, "the law was given by Moses, grace and truth came by Jesus Christ;" and the gifts granted through a faithful servant are not equal to those bestowed by the true Son. If then the law of Moses had been sufficient to confer eternal life, it were to no purpose for the Savior Himself to come and suffer for us, accomplishing the course of human life from His birth to His cross; and to no purpose for him who had done all the commandments of the law from his youth to fall on his knees and beg from another immortality. For he had not only fulfilled the law, but had begun to do so from his very earliest youth. For what is there great or pre-eminently illustrious in an old age which is unproductive of faults? But if one in juvenile frolicsomeness and the fire of youth shows a mature judgment older than his years, this is a champion admirable and distinguished, and hoary pre-eminently in mind. But, nevertheless, this man being such, is perfectly persuaded that nothing is wanting to him as far as respects righteousness, but that he is entirely destitute of life. Wherefore he asks it from Him who alone is able to give it. And with reference to the law, he carries confidence; but the Son of God he addresses in supplication. He is transferred from faith to faith. As perilously tossing and occupying a dangerous anchorage in the law, he makes for the Savior to find a haven.

IX. Jesus, accordingly, does not charge him with not having fulfilled all things out of the law, but loves him, and fondly welcomes his obedience in what he had learned; but says that he is not perfect as respects eternal life, inasmuch as he had not fulfilled what is perfect, and that he is a doer indeed of the law, but idle at the true life. Those things, indeed, are good. Who denies it? For "the commandment is holy," as far as a sort of training with fear and preparatory discipline goes, leading as it did to the culmination of legislation and to grace. But Christ is the fulfillment "of the law for righteousness to everyone that believeth;" and not as a slave making slaves, but sons, and brethren, and fellow-heirs, who perform the Father's will.

X. "If thou wilt be perfect." Consequently he was not yet perfect. For nothing is more perfect than what is perfect. And divinely the expression "if thou wilt" showed the self-determination of the soul holding converse with Him. For choice depended on the man as being free; but the gift on God as the Lord. And He gives to those who are willing and are exceedingly earnest, and ask, that so their salvation may become their own. For God compels not (for compulsion is repugnant to God), but supplies to those who seek, and bestows on those who ask, and opens to those who knock. If thou wilt, then, if thou really willest, and art not deceiving thyself, acquire what thou lackest. One thing is lacking thee, —the one thing which abides, the good, that which is now above the law, which the law gives not, which the law contains not, which is the prerogative of those who live. He forsooth who had fulfilled all the demands of the law from his youth, and had gloried in what was magnificent, was not able to complete the whole with this one thing which was specially required by the Savior, so as to receive the eternal life which he desired. But he departed displeased, vexed at the commandment of the life, on account of which he supplicated. For he did not truly wish life, as he averred, but aimed at the mere reputation of the good choice. And he was capable of busying himself about many things; but the one thing, the work of life, he was powerless, and disinclined, and unable to accomplish. Such also was what the Lord said to Martha, who was occupied with many things, and distracted and troubled with serving; while she blamed her sister, because, leaving serving, she set herself at His feet, devoting her time to learning: "Thou art troubled about many things, but Mary hath chosen the good part, which shall not be taken away from her." So also He bade him leave his busy life, and cleave to One and adhere to the grace of Him who offered everlasting life.

XI. What then was it which persuaded him to flight, and made him depart from the Master, from the entreaty, the hope, the life, previously pursued with ardor? — "Sell thy possessions." And what is this? He does not, as some conceive off-hand, bid him throw away the substance he possessed, and abandon his property; but bids him banish from his soul his notions about wealth, his excitement and morbid feeling about it, the anxieties, which are the thorns of existence, which choke the seed of life. For it is no great thing or desirable to be destitute of wealth, if without a special object, —not except on account of life. For thus those who have nothing at all, but are destitute, and beggars for their daily bread, the poor dispersed on the streets, who know not God and God's righteousness, simply on account of their extreme want and destitution of subsistence, and lack even of the smallest things, were most blessed and most dear to God, and sole possessors of everlasting life.

Nor was the renunciation of wealth and the bestowment of it on the poor or needy a new thing; for many did so before the Savior's advent, —some because of the leisure (thereby obtained) for learning, and on account of a dead wisdom; and others for empty fame and vainglory, as the Anaxagorases, the Democriti, and the Crateses.

XII. Why then command as new, as divine, as alone life-giving, what did not save those of former days? And what peculiar thing is it that the new creature the Son of God intimates and teaches? It is not the outward act which others have done, but something else indicated by it, greater, more godlike, more perfect, the stripping off of the passions from the soul itself and from the disposition, and the cutting up by the roots and casting out of what is alien to the mind. For this is the lesson peculiar to the believer, and the instruction worthy of the Savior. For those who formerly despised external things relinquished and squandered their property, but the passions of the soul, I believe, they intensified. For they indulged in arrogance, pretension, and vainglory, and in contempt of the rest of mankind, as if they had done something superhuman. How then would the Savior have enjoined on those destined to live forever what was injurious and hurtful with reference to the life which He promised? For although such is the case, one, after ridding himself of the burden of wealth, may none the less have still the lust and desire for money innate and living; and may have abandoned the use of it, but being at once destitute of and desiring what he spent, may doubly grieve both on account of the absence of attendance, and the presence of regret. For it is impossible and inconceivable that those in want of the necessaries of life should not be harassed in mind, and hindered from better things in the endeavor to provide them somehow, and from some source.

XIII. And how much more beneficial the opposite case, for a man, through possessing a competency, both not himself to be in straits about money, and also to give assistance to those to whom it is requisite so to do! For if no one had anything, what room would be left among men for giving? And how can this dogma fail to be found plainly opposed to and conflicting with many other excellent teachings of the Lord? "Make to yourselves friends of the mammon of unrighteousness, that when ye fail, they may receive you into the everlasting habitations." "Acquire treasures in heaven, where neither moth nor rust destroys, nor thieves break through." How could one give food to the hungry, and drink to the thirsty, clothe the naked, and shelter the houseless, for not doing which He threatens with fire and the outer darkness, if each man first divested himself of all these things? Nay, He bids Zaccheus and Matthew, the rich tax-gathers, entertain Him hospitably. And He does not bid them part with their property, but, applying the just and removing the unjust judgment, He subjoins, "To-day salvation has come to this house, forasmuch as he also is a son of Abraham." He so praises the use of property as to enjoin, along with this addition, the giving a share of it, to give drink to the thirsty, bread to the hungry, to take the houseless in, and clothe the naked. But if it is not possible to supply those needs without substance, and He bids people abandon their substance, what else would the Lord be doing than exhorting to give and not to give the same things, to feed and not to feed, to take in and to shut out, to share and not to share? Which were the most irrational of all things.

XIV. Riches, then, which benefit also our neighbors, are not to be thrown away. For they are possessions, inasmuch as they are possessed, and goods, inasmuch as they are useful and provided by God for the use of men; and they lie to our hand, and are put under our power, as material and instruments which are for good use to those who know the instrument.
If you use it skillfully, it is skilful; if you are deficient in skill, it is affected by your want of skill, being itself destitute of blame. Such an instrument is wealth. Are you able to make a right use of it? It is subservient to righteousness. Does one make a wrong use of it? It is, on the other hand, a minister of wrong. For its nature is to be subservient, not to rule. That then which of itself has neither good nor evil, being blameless, ought not to be blamed; but that which has the power of using it well and ill, by reason of its possessing voluntary choice. And this is the mind and judgment of man, which has freedom in itself and self-determination in the treatment of what is assigned to it. So let no man destroy wealth, rather than the passions of the soul, which are incompatible with the better use of wealth. So that, becoming virtuous and good, he may be able

to make a good use of these riches. The renunciation, then, and selling of all possessions, is to be understood as spoken of the passions of the soul.

XV. I would then say this. Since some things are within and some without the soul, and if the soul make a good use of them, they also are reputed good, but if a bad, bad; — whether does He who commands us to alienate our possessions repudiate those things, after the removal of which the passions still remain, or those rather, on the removal of which wealth even becomes beneficial? If therefore he who casts away worldly wealth can still be rich in the passions, even though the material [for their gratification] is absent, —for the disposition produces its own effects, and strangles the reason, and presses it down and inflames it with its inbred lusts, —it is then of no advantage to him to be poor in purse while he is rich in passions. For it is not what ought to be cast away that he has cast away, but what is indifferent; and he has deprived himself of what is serviceable, but set on fire the innate fuel of evil through want of the external means [of gratification]. We must therefore renounce those possessions that are injurious, not those that are capable of being serviceable, if one knows the right use of them. And what is managed with wisdom, and sobriety, and piety, is profit able; and what is hurtful must be cast away. But things external hurt not. So then the Lord introduces the use of external things, bidding us put away not the means of subsistence, but what uses them badly. And these are the infirmities and passions of the soul.

XVI. The presence of wealth in these is deadly to all, the loss of it salutary. Of which, making the soul pure, —that is, poor and bare, —we must hear the Savior speaking thus, "Come, follow Me." For to the pure in heart He now becomes the way. But into the impure soul the grace of God finds no entrance. And that (soul) is unclean which is rich in lusts, and is in the throes of many worldly affections. For he who holds possessions, and gold, and silver, and houses, as the gifts of God; and ministers from them to the God who gives them for the salvation of men; and knows that he possesses them more for the sake of the brethren than his own; and is superior to the possession of them, not the slave of the things he possesses; and does not carry them about in his soul, nor bind and circumscribe his life within them, but is ever laboring at some good and divine work, even should he be necessarily some time or other deprived of them, is able with cheerful mind to bear their removal equally with their abundance. This is he who is blessed by the Lord, and called poor in spirit, a meet heir of the kingdom of heaven, not one who could not live rich.

XVII. But he who carries his riches in his soul, and instead of God's Spirit bears in his heart gold or land, and is always acquiring possessions without end, and is perpetually on the outlook for more, bending downwards and fettered in the toils of the world, being earth and destined to depart to earth,—whence can he be able to desire and to mind the kingdom of heaven,—a man who carries not a heart, but land or metal, who must perforce be found in the midst of the objects he has chosen? For where the mind of man is, there is also his treasure. The Lord acknowledges a twofold treasure,— the good: "For the good man, out of the good treasure of his heart, bringeth forth good;" and the evil: for "the evil man, out of the evil treasure, bringeth forth evil: for out of the abundance of the heart the mouth speaketh." As then treasure is not one with Him, as also it is with us, that which gives the unexpected great gain in the finding, but also a second, which is profitless and undesirable, an evil acquisition, hurtful; so also there is a richness in good things, and a richness in bad things, since we know that riches and treasure are not by nature separated from each other. And the one sort of riches is to be possessed and acquired, and the other not to be possessed, but to be cast away. In the same way spiritual poverty is blessed. Wherefore also Matthew added, "Blessed are the poor." How? "In spirit." And again, "Blessed are they that hunger and thirst after the righteousness of God." Wherefore wretched are the contrary kind of poor, who have no part in God, and still less in human property, and have not tasted of the righteousness of God.

XVIII. So that (the expression) rich men that shall with difficulty enter into the kingdom, is to be apprehended in a scholarly way, not awkwardly, or rustically, or carnally. For if the expression is used thus, salvation does not depend on external things, whether they be many or few, small or great, or illustrious or obscure, or esteemed or disesteemed; but on the virtue of the soul, on faith, and hope, and love, and brotherliness, and knowledge, and meekness, and humility, and truth, the reward of which is salvation. For it is not on account of comeliness of body that any one shall live, or, on the other hand, perish. But he who uses the body given to him chastely and according to God, shall live; and he that destroys the temple of God shall be destroyed. An ugly man can be profligate, and a good-looking man temperate. Neither strength and great size of body makes alive, nor does any of the members destroy. But the soul which uses them provides the cause for each. Bear then, it is said, when struck on the face; which a man strong and in good health can obey. And again, a man who is feeble may transgress from refractoriness of temper. So also a poor and destitute man may be found intoxicated with lusts; and a man rich in worldly goods temperate, poor in indulgences, trustworthy, intelligent, pure, chastened. If then it is the soul which, first and especially, is that which is to live, and if virtue springing up around it saves, and vice kills; then it is clearly manifest that by being poor in those things, by riches of which one destroys it, it is saved, and by being rich in those things, riches of which ruin it, it is killed. And let us no longer seek the cause of the issue elsewhere than in the state and disposition of the soul in respect of obedience to God and purity, and in respect of transgression of the commandments and accumulation of wickedness.

XIX. He then is truly and rightly rich who is rich in virtue, and is capable of making a holy and faithful use of any fortune; while he is spuriously rich who is rich, according to the flesh, and turns life into outward possession, which is transitory and perishing, and now belongs to one, now to another, and in the end to nobody at all. Again, in the same way there is a genuine poor man, and another counterfeit and falsely so called. He that is poor in spirit, and that is the right thing, and he that is poor in a worldly sense, which is a different thing. To him who is poor in worldly goods, but rich in vices, who is not poor in spirit and rich toward God, it is said, Abandon the alien possessions that are in thy soul, that, becoming pure in heart, thou mayest see God; which is another way of saying, Enter into the kingdom of heaven. And how may you abandon them? By selling them. What then? Are you to take money for effects, by effecting an exchange of riches, by turning your visible substance into money? Not at all. But by introducing, instead of what was formerly inherent in your soul, which you desire to save, other riches which deify and which minister everlasting life, dispositions in accordance with the command of God; for which there shall accrue to you endless reward and honor, and salvation, and everlasting immortality. It is thus that thou dost rightly sell the possessions, many are superfluous, which shut the heavens against thee by exchanging them for those which are able to save. Let the former be possessed by the carnal poor, who are destitute of the latter. But thou, by receiving instead spiritual wealth, shalt have now treasure in the heavens.

XX. The wealthy and legally correct man, not understanding these things figuratively, nor how the same man can be both poor and rich, and have wealth and not have it, and use the world and not use it, went away sad and downcast, leaving the state of life, which he was able merely to desire but not to attain, making for himself the difficult impossible. For it was difficult for the soul not to be seduced and ruined by the luxuries and flowery enchantments that beset remarkable wealth; but it was not impossible, even surrounded with it, for one to lay hold of salvation, provided he withdrew himself from material wealth, —to that which is grasped by the mind and taught by God, and learned to use things indifferent rightly and properly, and so as to strive after eternal life. And the disciples even themselves were at first alarmed and amazed. Why were they so on hearing this? Was it that they themselves possessed much wealth? Nay, they had long ago left their very nets, and hooks, and rowing boats, which were their sole possessions. Why then do they say in consternation, "Who can be saved?" They had heard well and like disciples what was spoken in parable and obscurely by the Lord, and perceived the depth of the words. For they were sanguine of salvation on the ground of their want of wealth. But when they became conscious of not having yet wholly renounced the passions (for they were neophytes and recently selected by the Savior), they were excessively astonished, and despaired of themselves no less than that rich man who clung so terribly to the wealth which he preferred to eternal life. It was therefore a fit subject for all fear on the disciples' part; if both he that possesses wealth and he that is teeming with passions were the rich, and these alike shall be expelled from the heavens. For salvation is the privilege of pure and passionless souls.

XXI. But the Lord replies, "Because what is impossible with men is possible with God." This again is full of great wisdom. For a man by himself working and toiling at freedom from passion achieves nothing. But if he plainly shows himself very desirous and earnest about this, he attains it by the addition of the power of God. For God conspires with willing souls. But if they abandon their eagerness, the spirit which is bestowed by God is also restrained. For to save the unwilling is the part of one exercising compulsion; but to save the willing, that of one showing grace. Nor does the kingdom of heaven belong to sleepers and sluggards, "but the violent take it by force." For this alone is commendable violence, to force God, and take life from God by force. And He, knowing those who persevere firmly, or rather violently, yields and grants. For God delights in being vanquished in such things.

Therefore on hearing those words, the blessed Peter, the chosen, the pre-eminent, the first of the disciples, for whom alone and Himself the Savior paid tribute, quickly seized and comprehended the saying. And what does he say? "Lo, we have left all and followed Thee." Now if by all he means his own property, he boasts of leaving four oboli perhaps in all, and forgets to show the kingdom of heaven to be their recompense. But if, casting away what we were now speaking of, the old mental possessions and soul diseases, they follow in the Master's footsteps, this now joins them to those who are to be enrolled in the heavens. For it is thus that one truly follows the Savior, by aiming at sinlessness and at His perfection, and adorning and composing the soul before it as a mirror, and arranging everything in all respects similarly.

XXII. "And Jesus answering said, Verily I say unto you, Whosoever shall leave what is his own, parents, and children, and wealth, for My sake and the Gospel's, shall receive a hundredfold." But let neither this trouble you, nor the still harder saying delivered in another place in the words, "Whoso hateth not father, and mother, and children, and his own life besides, cannot be My disciple." For the God of peace, who also exhorts to love enemies, does not introduce hatred and dissolution from those that are dearest. But if we are to love our enemies, it is in accordance with right reason that, ascending from them, we should love also those nearest in kindred. Or if we are to hate our blood-relations, deduction teaches us that much more are we to spurn from us our enemies. So that the reasonings would be shown to destroy one another. But they do not destroy each other, nor are they near doing so. For from the same feeling and disposition, and on the ground of the same rule, one loving his enemy may hate his father, inasmuch as he neither takes vengeance on an enemy, nor reverences a father more than Christ. For by the one word he extirpates hatred and injury, and by the other shamefacedness towards one's relations, if it is detrimental to salvation. If then one's father, or son, or brother, be godless, and become a hindrance to faith and an impediment to the higher life, let him not be friends or agree with him, but on account of the spiritual enmity, let him dissolve the fleshly relationship.

XXIII. Suppose the matter to be a law-suit. Let your father be imagined to present himself to you and say, "I begot and reared thee. Follow me, and join with me in wickedness, and obey not the law of Christ;" and whatever a man who is a blasphemer and dead by nature would say.

But on the other side hear the Savior: "I regenerated thee, who wert ill born by the world to death. I emancipated, healed, ransomed thee. I will show thee the face of the good Father God. Call no man thy father on earth. Let the dead bury the dead; but follow thou Me. For I will bring thee to a rest of ineffable and unutterable blessings, which eye hath not seen, nor ear heard, nor have entered into the heart of men; into which angels desire to look, and see what good things God hath prepared for the saints and the children who love Him." I am He who feeds thee, giving Myself as bread, of which he who has tasted experiences death no more, and supplying day by day the drink of immortality. I am teacher of supercelestial lessons. For thee I contended with Death, and paid thy death, which thou owedst for thy former sins and thy unbelief towards God."

Having heard these considerations on both sides, decide for thyself and give thy vote for thine own salvation. Should a brother say the like, should a child, should a wife, should any one whosoever, in preference to all let Christ in thee be conqueror. For He contends in thy behalf.

XXIV. You may even go against wealth. Say, "Certainly Christ does not debar me from property. The Lord does not envy." But do you see yourself overcome and overthrown by it? Leave it, throw it away, hate, renounce, flee. "Even if thy right eye offend thee," quickly "cut it out." Better is the kingdom of God to a man with one eye, than the fire to one who is unmutilated. Whether hand, or foot, or soul, hate it.

For if it is destroyed here for Christ's sake, it will be restored to life yonder.

XXV. And to this effect similarly is what follows. "Now at this present time not to have lands, and money, and houses, and brethren, with persecutions." For it is neither penniless, nor homeless, nor brotherless people that the Lord calls to life, since He has also called rich people; but, as we have said above, also brothers, as Peter with Andrew, and James with John the sons of Zebedee, but of one mind with each other and Christ. And the expression "with persecutions" rejects the possessing of each of those things. There is a persecution which arises from without, from men assailing the faithful, either out of hatred, or envy, or avarice, or through diabolic agency. But the most painful is internal persecution, which proceeds from each man's own soul being vexed by impious lusts, and diverse pleasures, and base hopes, and destructive dreams; when, always grasping at more, and maddened by brutish loves, and inflamed by the passions which beset it like goads and stings, it is covered with blood, (to drive it on) to insane pursuits, and to despair of life, and to contempt of God.

More grievous and painful is this persecution, which arises from within, which is ever with a man, and which the persecuted cannot escape; for he carries the enemy about everywhere in himself. Thus also burning which attacks from without works trial, but that from within produces death. War also made on one is easily put an end to, but that which is in the soul continues till death.

With such persecution, if you have worldly wealth, if you have brothers allied by blood and other pledges, abandon the whole wealth of these which leads to evil; procure peace for yourself, free yourself from protracted persecutions; turn from them to the Gospel; choose before all the Savior and Advocate and Paraclete of your soul, the Prince of life. "For the things which are seen are temporary; but the things which are not seen are eternal." And in the present time are things evanescent and insecure, but in that to come is eternal life.

XXVI. "The first shall be last, and the last first." This is fruitful in meaning and exposition, but does not demand investigation at present; for it refers not only to the wealthy alone, but plainly to all men, who have once surrendered themselves to faith. So let this stand aside for the present. But I think that our proposition has been demonstrated in no way inferior to what we promised, that the Savior by no means has excluded the rich on account of wealth itself, and the possession of property, nor fenced off salvation against them; if they are able and willing to submit their life to God's commandments, and prefer them to transitory objects, and if they would look to the Lord with steady eye, as those who look for the nod of a good helmsman, what he wishes, what he orders, what he indicates, what signal he gives his mariners, where and whence he directs the ship's course. For what harm does one do, who, previous to faith, by applying his mind and by saving has collected a competency? Or what is much less reprehensible than this, if at once by God, who gave him his life, he has had his home given him in the house of such men, among wealthy people, powerful in substance, and pre-eminent in opulence? For if, in consequence of his involuntary birth in wealth, a man is banished from life, rather is he wronged by God, who created him, in having vouchsafed to him temporary enjoyment, and in being deprived of eternal life. And why should wealth have ever sprung from the earth at all, if it is the author and patron of death?

But if one is able in the midst of wealth to turn from its power, and to entertain moderate sentiments, and to exercise self-command, and to seek God alone, and to breathe God and walk with God, such a poor man submits to the commandments, being free, unsubdued, free of disease, unwounded by wealth. But if not, "sooner shall a camel enter through a needle's eye, than such a rich man reach the kingdom of God."

Let then the camel, going through a narrow and strait way before the rich man, signify something loftier; which mystery of the Savior is to be learned in the "Exposition of first Principles and of Theology."

XXVII. Well, first let the point of the parable, which is evident, and the reason why it is spoken, be presented. Let it teach the prosperous that they are not to neglect their own salvation, as if they had been already fore-doomed, nor, on the other hand, to cast wealth into the sea, or condemn it as a traitor and an enemy to life, but learn in what way and how to use wealth and obtain life. For since neither does one perish by any means by fearing because he is rich, nor is by any means saved by trusting and believing that he shall be saved, come let them look what hope the Savior assigns them, and how what is unexpected may become ratified, and what is hoped for may come into possession.

The Master accordingly, when asked, "Which is the greatest of the commandments?" says, "Thou shalt love the Lord thy God with all thy soul, and with all thy strength;" that no commandment is greater than this (He says), and with exceeding good reason; for it gives command respecting the First and the Greatest, God Himself, our Father, by whom all things were brought into being, and exist, and to whom what is saved returns again. By Him, then, being loved beforehand, and having received existence, it is impious for us to regard aught else older or more excellent; rendering only this small tribute of gratitude for the greatest benefits; and being unable to imagine anything else whatever by way of recompense to God, who needs nothing and is perfect; and gaining immortality by the very exercise of loving the Father to the extent of one's might and power. For the more one loves God, the more he enters within God.

XXVIII. The second in order, and not any less than this, He says, is, "Thou shalt love thy neighbor as thyself," consequently God above thyself. And on His interlocutor inquiring, "Who is my neighbor?" He did not, in the same way with the Jews, specify the blood-relation, or the fellow-citizen, or the proselyte, or him that had been similarly circumcised, or the man who uses one and the same law. But He introduces one on his way down from the upland region from Jerusalem to Jericho, and represents him stabbed by robbers, cast half-dead on the way, passed by the priest, looked sideways at by the Levite, but pitied by the vilified and excommunicated Samaritan; who did not, like those, pass casually, but came provided with such things as the man in danger required, such as oil, bandages, a beast of burden, money for the inn-keeper, part given now, and part promised. "Which," said He, "of them was neighbor to him that suffered these things?" and on his answering, "He that showed mercy to him," (replied), Go thou also, therefore, and do likewise, since love buds into well-doing.

XXIX. In both the commandments, then, He introduces love; but in order distinguishes it. And in the one He assigns to God the first part of love, and allots the second to our neighbor. Who else can it be but the Savior Himself? or who more than He has pitied us, who by the rulers of darkness were all but put to death with many wounds, fears, lusts, passions, pains, deceits, pleasures? Of these wounds the only physician is Jesus, who cuts out the passions thoroughly by the root, —not as the law does the bare effects, the fruits of evil plants, but applies His axe to the roots of wickedness. He it is that poured wine on our wounded souls (the blood of David's vine), that brought the oil which flows from the compassions of the Father, and bestowed it copiously. He it is that produced the ligatures of health and of salvation that cannot be undone, —Love, Faith, Hope. He it is that subjected angels, and principalities, and powers, for a great reward to serve us. For they also shall be delivered from the vanity of the world through the revelation of the glory of the sons of God. We are therefore to love Him equally with God. And he loves Christ Jesus who does His will and keeps His commandments. "For not everyone that saith unto Me, Lord, Lord, shall enter into the kingdom of heaven;

but he that doeth the will of My Father." And "Why call ye Me Lord, Lord, and do not the things which I say?" "And blessed are ye who see and hear what neither righteous men nor prophets" (have seen or heard), if ye do what I say.

XXX. He then is first who loves Christ; and second, he who loves and cares for those who have believed on Him. For whatever is done to a disciple, the Lord accepts as done to Himself, and reckons the whole as His. "Come, ye blessed of My Father, inherit the kingdom prepared for you from the foundation of the world. For I was a hungered, and ye gave Me to eat: I was thirsty, and ye gave Me to drink: and I was a stranger, and ye took Me in: I was naked and ye clothed Me: I was sick, and ye visited Me: I was in prison, and ye came to Me. Then shall the righteous answer, saying, Lord, when saw we Thee hungry, and fed Thee? Or thirsty, and gave Thee drink? And when saw we Thee a stranger, and took Thee in? or naked, and clothed Thee? Or when saw we Thee sick, and visited Thee? or in prison, and came to Thee? And the King answering, shall say to them, Verily I say unto you, inasmuch as ye have done it unto one of the least of these My brethren, ye have done it unto Me."

Again, on the opposite side, to those who have not performed these things, "Verily I say unto you, inasmuch as ye have not done it unto one of the least of these, ye have not done it to Me." And in another place, "He that receiveth you; receiveth Me; and he that receiveth not you, rejecteth Me."

XXXI. Such He names children, and sons, and little children, and friends, and little ones here, in reference to their future greatness above. "Despise not," He says, "one of these little ones; for their angels always behold the face of My Father in heaven." And in another place, "Fear not, little flock, for it is your Father's good pleasure to give you the kingdom of heaven." Similarly also He says that "the least in the kingdom of heaven" that is His own disciple "is greater than John, the greatest among those born of women." And again, "He that receiveth a righteous man or a prophet in the name of a righteous man or a prophet, shall receive their reward; and he that giveth to a disciple in the name of a disciple a cup of cold water to drink, shall not lose his reward." Wherefore this is the only reward that is not lost. And again, "Make to you friends of the mammon of unrighteousness, that, when ye fail, they may receive you into everlasting habitations;" showing that by nature all property which a man possesses in his own power is not his own. And from this unrighteousness it is permitted to work a righteous and saving thing, to refresh some one of those who have an everlasting habitation with the Father.

See then, first, that He has not commanded you to be solicited or to wait to be importuned, but yourself to seek those who are to be benefited and are worthy disciples of the Savior. Excellent, accordingly, also is the apostle's saying, "For the Lord loveth a cheerful giver;" who delights in giving, and spares not, sowing so that he may also thus reap, without murmuring, and disputing, and regret, and communicating, which is pure beneficence. But better than this is the saying spoken by the Lord in another place, "Give to everyone that asketh thee." For truly such is God's delight in giving. And this saying is above all divinity, —not to wait to be asked, but to inquire oneself who deserves to receive kindness.

XXXII. Then to appoint such a reward for liberality, — an everlasting habitation! O excellent trading! O divine merchandise! One purchases immortality for money; and, by giving the perishing things of the world, receives in exchange for these an eternal mansion in the heavens! Sail to this mart, if you are wise, O rich man! If need be, sail around the whole world. Spare not perils and toils, that you may purchase here the heavenly kingdom. Why do transparent stones and emeralds delight thee so much, and a house that is fuel for fire, or a plaything of time, or the sport of the earthquake, or an occasion for a tyrant's outrage? Aspire to dwell in the heavens, and to reign with God. This kingdom a man imitating God will give thee. By receiving a little here, there through all ages He will make thee a dweller with Him. Ask that you may receive;

haste; strive; fear lest He disgrace thee. For He is not commanded to receive, but thou to give. The Lord did not say, Give, or bring, or do good, or help, but make a friend. But a friend proves himself such not by one gift, but by long intimacy. For it is neither the faith, nor the love, nor the hope, nor the endurance of one day, but "he that endureth to the end shall be saved."

XXXIII. How then does man give these things? For I will give not only to friends, but to the friends of friends. And who is it that is the friend of God? Do not you judge who is worthy or who is unworthy. For it is possible you may be mistaken in your opinion. As in the uncertainty of ignorance it is better to do good to the undeserving for the sake of the deserving, than by guarding against those that are less good to fail to meet in with the good. For though sparing, and aiming at testing, who will receive meritoriously or not, it is possible for you to neglect some that are loved by God; the penalty for which is the punishment of eternal fire. But by offering to all in turn that need, you must of necessity by all means find some one of those who have power with God to save. "Judge not, then, that ye be not judged. With what measure ye mete, it shall be measured to you again; good measure, pressed and shaken, and running over, shall be given to you." Open thy compassion to all who are enrolled the disciples of God; not looking contemptuously to personal appearance, nor carelessly disposed to any period of life. Nor if one appears penniless, or ragged, or ugly, or feeble, do thou fret in soul at this and turn away. This form is cast around us from without, the occasion of our entrance into this world, that we may be able to enter into this common school. But within dwells the hidden Father, and His Son, who died for us and rose with us.

XXXIV. This visible appearance cheats death and the devil; for the wealth within, the beauty, is unseen by them. And they rave about the carcase, which they despise as weak, being blind to the wealth within; knowing not what a "treasure in an earthen vessel" we bear, protected as it is by the power of God the Father, and the blood of God the Son, and the dew of the Holy Spirit. But be not deceived, thou who hast tasted of the truth, and been reckoned worthy of the great redemption. But contrary to what is the case with the rest of men, collect for thyself an unarmed, an unwarlike, a bloodless, a passionless, a stainless host, pious old men, orphans dear to God, widows armed with meekness, men, adorned with love. Obtain with thy money such guards, for body and for soul, for whose sake a sinking ship is made buoyant, when steered by the prayers of the saints alone; and disease at its height is subdued, put to flight by the laying on of hands; and the attack of robbers is disarmed, spoiled by pious prayers; and the might of demons is crushed, put to shame in its operations by strenuous commands.

XXXV. All these warriors and guards are trusty. No one is idle, no one is useless. One can obtain your pardon from God, another comfort you when sick, another weep and groan in sympathy for you to the Lord of all, another teach some of the things useful for salvation, another admonish with confidence, another counsel with kindness. And all can love truly, without guile, without fear, without hypocrisy, without flattery, without pretence. O sweet service of loving [souls]! O blessed thoughts of confident [hearts]! O sincere faith of those who fear God alone! O truth of words with those who cannot lie! O beauty of deeds with those who have been commissioned to serve God, to persuade God, to please God, not to touch thy flesh! to speak, but to the King of eternity dwelling in thee.

XXXVI. All the faithful, then, are good and godlike, and worthy of the name by which they are encircled as with a diadem. There are, besides, some, the elect of the elect, and so much more or less distinguished by drawing themselves, like ships to the strand, out of the surge of the world and bringing themselves to safety; not wishing to seem holy, and ashamed if one call them so; hiding in the depth of their mind the ineffable mysteries, and disdaining to let their nobleness be seen in the world; whom the Word calls "the light of the world, and the salt of the earth." This is the seed, the image and likeness of

God, and His true son and heir, sent here as it were on a sojourn, by the high administration and suitable arrangement of the Father, by whom the visible and invisible things of the world were created; some for their service, some for their discipline, some for their instruction; and all things are held together so long as the seed remains here; and when it is gathered, these things shall be very quickly dissolved.

XXXVII. For what further need has God of the mysteries of love? And then thou shalt look into the bosom of the Father, whom God the only-begotten Son alone hath declared. And God Himself is love; and out of love to us became feminine. In His ineffable essence He is Father; in His compassion to us He became Mother. The Father by loving became feminine: and the great proof of this is He whom He begot of Himself; and the fruit brought forth by love is love.

For this also He came down. For this He clothed Himself with man. For this He voluntarily subjected Himself to the experiences of men, that by bringing Himself to the measure of our weakness whom He loved, He might correspondingly bring us to the measure of His own strength. And about to be offered up and giving Himself a ransom, He left for us a new Covenant-testament: My love I give unto you. And what and how great is it? For each of us He gave His life, —the equivalent for all. This He demands from us in return for one another. And if we owe our lives to the brethren, and have made such a mutual compact with the Savior, why should we any more hoard and shut up worldly goods, which are beggarly, foreign to us and transitory? Shall we shut up from each other what after a little shall be the property of the fire? Divinely and weightily John says, "He that loveth not his brother is a murderer," the seed of Cain, a nursling of the devil. He has not God's compassion. He has no hope of better things. He is sterile; he is barren; he is not a branch of the ever-living supercelestial vine. He is cut off; he waits the perpetual fire.

XXXVIII. But learn thou the more excellent way, which Paul shows for salvation. "Love seeketh not her own," but is diffused on the brother. About him she is fluttered, about him she is soberly insane. "Love covers a multitude of sins." "Perfect love casteth out fear." "Vaunted not itself, is not puffed up; rejoiceth not in iniquity, but rejoiceth in the truth; beareth all things, believeth all things, hopeth all things, endureth all things. Love never faileth. Prophecies are done away, tongues cease, gifts of healing fail on the earth. But these three abide, Faith, Hope, Love. But the greatest of these is Love." And rightly. For Faith departs when we are convinced by vision, by seeing God. And Hope vanishes when the things hoped for come. But Love comes to completion, and grows more when that which is perfect has been bestowed. If one introduces it into his soul, although he be born in sins, and has done many forbidden things, he is able, by increasing love, and adopting a pure repentance, to retrieve his mistakes. For let not this be left to despondency and despair by you, if you learn who the rich man is that has not a place in heaven, and what way he uses his property.

XXXIX. If one should escape the superfluity of riches, and the difficulty they interpose in the way of life, and be able to enjoy the eternal good things; but should happen, either from ignorance or involuntary circumstances, after the seal and redemption, to fall into sins or transgressions so as to be quite carried away; such a man is entirely rejected by God. For to everyone who has turned to God in truth, and with his whole heart, the doors are open, and the thrice-glad Father receives His truly repentant son. And true repentance is to be no longer bound in the same sins for which He denounced death against Himself, but to eradicate them completely from the soul. For on their extirpation God takes up His abode again in thee. For it is said there is great and exceeding joy and festival in the heavens with the Father and the angels when one sinner turns and repents. Wherefore also He cries, "I will have mercy, and not sacrifice." "I desire not the death, but the repentance of the sinner." "Though your sins be as scarlet wool, I will make them white as snow; though they be blacker than darkness, I will wash and make them like white wool." For it is in the power of God alone to grant the forgiveness of sins, and not to impute transgressions; since also the Lord commands us each day to forgive the repenting brethren. "And if we, being evil, know to give good gifts," much more is it the nature of the Father of mercies, the good Father of all consolation, much pitying, very merciful, to be long-suffering, to wait for those who have turned. And to turn is really to cease from our sins, and to look no longer behind.

XL. Forgiveness of past sins, then, God gives; but of future, each one gives to himself. And this is to repent, to condemn the past deeds, and beg oblivion of them from the Father, who only of all is able to undo what is done, by mercy proceeding from Him, and to blot out former sins by the dew of the Spirit. "For by the state in which I find you will I judge," also, is what in each case the end of all cries aloud. So that even in the case of one who has done the greatest good deeds in his life, but at the end has run headlong into wickedness, all his former pains are profitless to him, since at the catastrophe of the drama he has given up his part; while it is possible for the man who formerly led a bad and dissolute life, on afterwards repenting, to overcome in the time after repentance the evil conduct of a long time. But it needs great carefulness, just as bodies that have suffered by protracted disease need regimen and special attention. Thief, dost thou wish to get forgiveness? steal no more. Adulterer, burn no more. Fornicator, live for the future chastely. Thou who hast robbed, give back, and give back more than [thou tookest]. False witness, practice truth. Perjurer, swear no more, and extirpate the rest of the passions, wrath, lust, grief, fear; that thou mayest be found at the end to have previously in this world been reconciled to the adversary.

It is then probably impossible all at once to eradicate inbred passions; but by God's power and human intercession, and the help of brethren, and sincere repentance, and constant care, they are corrected.

XLI. Wherefore it is by all means necessary for thee, who art pompous, and powerful, and rich, to set over thyself some man of God as a trainer and governor. Reverence, though it be but one man; fear, though it be but one man. Give yourself to hearing, though it be but one speaking freely, using harshness, and at the same time healing. For it is good for the eyes not to continue always wanton, but to weep and smart sometimes, for greater health. So also nothing is more pernicious to the soul than uninterrupted pleasure. For it is blinded by melting away, if it remain unmoved by bold speech. Fear this man when angry; be pained at his groaning; and reverence him when making his anger to cease; and anticipate him when he is deprecating punishment. Let him pass many sleepless nights for thee, interceding for thee with God, influencing the Father with the magic of familiar litanies. For He does not hold out against His children when they beg His pity. And for you he will pray purely, held in high honor as an angel of God, and grieved not by you, but for you. This is sincere repentance. "God is not mocked," nor does He give heed to vain words. For He alone searches the marrow and reins of the heart, and hears those that are in the fire, and listens to those who supplicate in the whale's belly; and is near to all who believe, and far from the ungodly if they repent not.

XLII. And that you may be still more confident, that repenting thus truly there remains for you a sure hope of salvation, listen to a tale, which is not a tale but a narrative, handed down and committed to the custody of memory, about the Apostle John. For when, on the tyrant's death, he returned to Ephesus from the isle of Patmos, he went away, being invited, to the contiguous territories of the nations, here to appoint bishops, there to set in order whole Churches, there to ordain such as were marked out by the Spirit. Having come to one of the cities not far off (the name of which some give), and having put the brethren to rest in other matters, at last, looking to the bishop appointed, and seeing a youth, powerful in body, comely in appearance, and ardent, said, "This (youth)

I commit to you in all earnestness, in the presence of the Church, and with Christ as witness." And on his accepting and promising all, he gave the same injunction and testimony. And he set out for Ephesus. And the presbyter taking home the youth committed to him, reared, kept, cherished, and finally baptized him. After this he relaxed his stricter care and guardianship, under the idea that the seal of the Lord he had set on him was a complete protection to him. But on his obtaining premature freedom, some youths of his age, idle, dissolute, and adepts in evil courses, corrupt him. First they entice him by many costly entertainments; then afterwards by night issuing forth for highway robbery, they take him along with them.

Then they dared to execute together something greater. And he by degrees got accustomed; and from greatness of nature, when he had gone aside from the right path, and like a hard mouthed and powerful horse, had taken the bit between his teeth, rushed with all the more force down into the depths. And having entirely despaired of salvation in God, he no longer meditated what was insignificant, but having perpetrated some great exploit, now that he was once lost, he made up his mind to a like fate with the rest. Taking them and forming a band of robbers, he was the prompt captain of the bandits, the fiercest, the bloodiest, the cruelest. Time passed, and some necessity having emerged, they send again for John. He, when he had settled the other matters on account of which he came, said, "Come now, O bishop, restore to us the deposit which I and the Savior committed to thee in the face of the Church over which you preside, as witness." The other was at first confounded, thinking that it was a false charge about money which he did not get; and he could neither believe the allegation regarding what he had not, nor disbelieve John. But when he said "I demand the young man, and the soul of the brother," the old man, groaning deeply, and bursting into tears, said, "He is dead." "How and what kind of death?" "He is dead," he said, "to God. For he turned wicked and abandoned, and at last a robber; and now he has taken possession of the mountain in front of the church, along with a band like him." Rending, therefore, his clothes, and striking his head with great lamentation, the apostle said, "It was a fine guard of a brother's soul I left! But let a horse be brought me, and let someone be my guide on the way." He rode away, just as he was, straight from the church. On coming to the place, he is arrested by the robbers' outpost; neither fleeing nor entreating, but crying, "It was for this I came. Lead me to your captain;" who meanwhile was waiting, all armed as he was. But when he recognized John as he advanced, he turned, ashamed, to flight. The other followed with all his might, forgetting his age, crying, "Why, my son, dost thou flee from me, thy father, unarmed, old? Son, pity me. Fear not; thou hast still hope of life. I will give account to Christ for thee. If need be, I will willingly endure thy death, as the Lord did death for us. For thee I will surrender my life. Stand, believe; Christ hath sent me."

And he, when he heard, first stood, looking down; then threw down his arms, then trembled and wept bitterly. And on the old man approaching, he embraced him, speaking for himself with lamentations as he could, and baptized a second time with tears, concealing only his right hand. The other pledging, and assuring him on oath that he would find forgiveness for himself from the Savior, beseeching and falling on his knees, and kissing his right hand itself, as now purified by repentance, led him back to the church. Then by supplicating with copious prayers, and striving along with him in continual fastings, and subduing his mind by various utterances of words, did not depart, as they say, till he restored him to the Church, presenting in him a great example of true repentance and a great token of regeneration, a trophy of the resurrection for which we hope; when at the end of the world, the angels, radiant with joy, hymning and opening the heavens, shall receive into the celestial abodes those who truly repent; and before all, the Savior Himself goes to meet them, welcoming them; holding forth the shadowless, ceaseless light;

conducting them, to the Father's bosom, to eternal life, to the kingdom of heaven.

Let one believe these things, and the disciples of God, and God, who is surety, the Prophecies, the Gospels, the Apostolic words; living in accordance with them, and lending his ears, and practicing the deeds, he shall at his decease see the end and demonstration of the truths taught. For he who in this world welcomes the angel of penitence will not repent at the time that he leaves the body, nor be ashamed when he sees the Savior approaching in His glory and with His army. He fears not the fire.

But if one chooses to continue and to sin perpetually in pleasures, and values indulgence here above eternal life, and turns away from the Savior, who gives forgiveness; let him no more blame either God, or riches, or his having fallen, but his own soul, which voluntarily perishes. But to him who directs his eye to salvation and desires it, and asks with boldness and vehemence for its bestowal, the good Father who is in heaven will give the true purification and the changeless life. To whom, by His Son Jesus Christ, the Lord of the living and dead, and by the Holy Spirit, be glory, honor, power, eternal majesty, both now and ever, from generation to generation, and from eternity to eternity. Amen.

Elucidations

I.
(Note 1, p. 591.)

The kingdom of Christ was set up in great weakness, that nothing might be wanting to the glory of His working by the Spirit, in its triumph over the darkness of the world. "Not many wise men after the flesh, not many mighty, not many noble," were called. And so it continued for a long time. Under Commodus, however (a.d. 180–192), a temporary respite was conceded; partly because his favorite Marcia took their part for some reason, and partly because his cruelty gratified itself in another direction. "Our circumstances," says Eusebius, "were changed to a milder aspect; as there was peace prevailing, by the grace of God, throughout the world in the churches. Then, also, the saving-doctrine brought the minds of men to a devout veneration of the Supreme God, from every race on earth, so that, now, many of those *eminent at Rome for their wealth and kindred, with their whole house and family*, yielded themselves to salvation." What happened near the court of a fickle tyrant was far more likely to be common in Antioch and Alexandria. Men's consciences had no doubt been with the Christians, as Pilate's was with their Master; and now, when it became less perilous, they began to laugh at idols, and even to enroll themselves with Christians. Some, no doubt, like Joseph and Nicodemus, gave themselves to the Lord; but others, "with a form of godliness, denied the power thereof." Clement detected the great evil that began to threaten, and this beautiful tract is the product of his watchful observation. For he was gifted, also, with that great characteristic of noble mind, a faculty of foreseeing "whereunto such things must grow." His love and solicitude for the Church, lest its simplicity should pass away with its poverty, dictated this solemn and most timely warning.

And it is worthy of grateful remark, how admirably sustained was this primitive spirit among all the early witnesses for truth. They were not of this world, and they dreaded its influence. How richly the Word dwelt in them, is manifest from their amazing familiarity with the Scriptures. That they sometimes misquote or confuse quotations, or mix a Scriptural saying with some current proverb or an apocryphal gloss, is surely not surprising, when copies of the Scriptures were few and costly, when no concordances and books of reference were at hand, and when their whole apparatus for Biblical study was so extremely incomplete. To the genius of this great Alexandrian Father, we are all debtors to this day. Had he not, unfortunately, allied much of his wisdom with the hateful name of the *Gnostic*, which he failed to wrest from the pseudo-Gnostics, with whom it is irrevocably associated, we may be sure his expositions of Christian philosophy would be more useful in our times.

II.
(Segaar, note 3, p. 594.)

Charles Segaar, S.T.D., born in 1724, was Greek professor at Utrecht, from 1766 to 1803, after filling several important and laborious positions as a pastor and preacher. He died Dec. 22, 1803. He has left a great reputation as "the most theological of philologists, and the most philological of theologians." Had he gone over the entire text of Clement, and edited all his works, with the care and ability displayed in his critical edition of the Τίς ὁ σωζόμενος πλούσιος, the world would have been greatly enriched by his influence on the cultivation of patristic literature. In his eloquent preface to this tract, he bewails the neglect into which that fundamental department of Christian learning had fallen; praising the labors of Anglican scholars, who, in the former century, had devoted themselves to the production of valuable editions of the Fathers. He speaks of himself as from early years inflamed with a singular love of such studies and especially of the Greek Fathers, and adds an expression of the extreme gratification with which he had read and pondered the *Quis dives Salvandus*, among the admirable works of Clement of Alexandria. He corrects Ghisler's error in crediting it to Origen (edition of 1623), and reminds us that there is but a single ms. from which it is derived, viz., that of the Vatican.

Apart from the value of Segaar's annotations, his work is very useful to Greek scholars, for its varied erudition, much wealth of his learning being expended upon single words and their idiomatic uses. The sort of work devoted to this tract is precisely what I covet for my countrymen; and I look forward with hope to the day as not remote, when from regions now unnamed, in this vast domain of our republican America, critical editions of all of the *Ante-Nicene Fathers* shall be given to the republic of letters, with a beauty of typography hitherto unknown. The valuable *Patrologia* of Migne might well be made the base of a Phoenix-like edition of the same series. It was only fit for such a base; for its print and paper are disgraceful, and the inaccuracy and carelessness of its references and editorial work are only pardonable when one reflects on the small cost at which it was afforded. The plates have perished in flames; but the restoration of the whole work is worthy of the ambition of American scholars, and of the patronage of wealth now sordid but capable of being ennobled by being made useful to mankind.

III.
(Willing Souls, cap. xxi. p. 597.)

On the subject of free-will, so profusely illustrated by Clement, I have foreborne to add any comments. But Segaar's *Excursus* (iv. p. 410) is worthy of being consulted. On Clement's ideas of *Hades* and the *intermediate state*, I have made no comment; but Segaar's endeavor to state judicially the view of our author (*Excursus*, x. p. 421), though in some particulars it seems to me unsatisfactory, is also worthy of examination. If a number of other important points have been apparently overlooked in my Elucidations, it is because I fear I have already gone beyond the conditions and limitations of my work.

www.ingramcontent.com/pod-product-compliance
Lightning Source LLC
Chambersburg PA
CBHW052043070526
44584CB00018B/2591